# Cool Women

## *Volume Six*

*poems*

Also by Cool Women

Anthologies

CD's

# Cool Women
## *Volume Six*
### *poems*

Eloise Bruce
Juditha Dowd
Lois Marie Harrod
Betty Bonham Lies
Judy Rowe Michaels
Sharon Olson
Penelope Scambly Schott
Maxine Susman
Gretna Wilkinson

COOL WOMEN PRESS
Hopewell, NJ 08525

Copyright © Cool Women 2016

Cover Photograph: *Spring Birch* © Jacki Dickert 2016, *www. lightdance.org*

Published by COOL WOMEN PRESS
111 Taylor Terrace
Hopewell, NJ 08525
https://coolwomenpoets.org/

To order contact:
COOL WOMEN PRESS
111 Taylor Terrace
Hopewell, NJ 08525
lmharrod1@verizon.net


Library of Congress Cataloguing-in-Publication Data
Bruce, Eloise
Dowd, Juditha
Harrod, Lois Marie
Lies, Betty Bonham
Michaels, Judy
Olson, Sharon
Schott, Penelope Scambly
Susman, Maxine
Wilkinson, Gretna

ISBN: 978-0-9707812-9-1
1. Title
2. Women's Studies
3. Poetry

Library of Congress Number 201694375

Nothing in this world seemed only one thing
and not another.
*Claire Keyes*


Women who let their dreams
curl at the end.
*Mary Ruefle*

# Table of Contents

## Muse-ings

## Knowing/Not Knowing

## Critters Like Us

## On Further Thought

## Beside Ourselves

Muse-ings

## Thinking Ahead

Maybe you discovered this poem in a dry cave
and now as you examine the yellowing paper

you are puzzling over the black scratch marks.
They could be hard to decipher like Linear B.

Maybe to you the *O*'s look like small ponds
and the *T*'s like the handles of antique daggers.

What sort of language do you speak? What if
your throat and mouth don't resemble ours?

It will have been such a long time. You might
be a child of whales who staggered ashore

from an acid sea. At night do you study stars?
Once when my father was old and left the city,

he asked me, *What is that white line in the sky?*
Maybe you have traveled beyond the farthest

edge of the Milky Way galaxy and finally come
back home to tell me all about it. I'm listening.

## Villanelle for My Brother

I'd like to hide you in a villanelle
for safekeeping. Less room for risk.
The music fits you well.

Form should give pleasure, not just build a shell
to house my hurt, conceal your darkening fear.
I'd like to grace you with a villanelle

that keeps you with me but removes the chill
years of knives, self-mutilation.
The music fits you well.

I often try to dream you back, unseal
the playful, witty mind I thought I knew.
How can I ask you in a villanelle

(slip between rhymes) to try to tell
me why? Why you had no other choice.
The music fits you well.

My bitter why, your creature-in-a-wheel
that only knew it had to end its whirl:
Can't I just love you in a villanelle
and stop the endless carousel?

*Gretna Wilkinson*

## Underground Jazz Continued

His tenor sax released a semibreve
that mistook time for eternity

*Take it*, he urged. *Light some fire*

And he restarted Sonny Rollins' *Shadrack*
aiming for smooth

Her horn seemed to swallow the note whole
like she was trying to out-Sonny the Rollins

*Play more like you,* he pressed, *outdo you*

When he resumed the song
she crawled inside the piece note upon note
like a stairway to a dream.
It made her toes sweat
as she tapped to tap it away.
Woman and horn were now
hardwired for rebellion

Just then, the sax freed a husky b flat
and a new sound stirred in the horn.
It pulled her behind this moment
to the one in her childhood
where she was drinking limeade
on the rickety back porch
and great grandmother
was telling secrets to dusk again, saying:

*Livin sho wadn easy. But hope keep acomin. keep
acomin. Sometime, it feel like God hisself be testin me.
Bluesin up me life. Jazzin up yestiday pain. Stuffin it in
de back pocket of tomorrah misry. Sometime, hope itself
get all funky too*

*Staywithmegirl!*

Startled, she pushed a string
of velvet-wrapped tones
that stirred Regular Reggie
leaning beside the door.
He caught his breath, daubed a tear
and stepped away from the juke joint
*I can smell tomorrow again,*
he whispered into the night.
Unaware that he had whispered

*Eloise Bruce*

# What Can Travel Faster than the Speed of Light?

*Right, if the CERN (OPERA Project) experiment proves to be correct
and neutrinos have broken the speed of light, I will eat my boxer shorts
on live TV.* Jim Al-Khalili, Professor of Theoretical Physics

The newest Italian OPERA begs the question.
What a difference sixty nanoseconds can make?
In the main plot, neutrinos have traveled from Switzerland to Italy
faster than the speed of light, and long-dead countryman
Galileo didn't actually know enough, but
even he rolled over in his grave and of course
Fermi, Pauli and Einstein flipped out and over.

In the cosmic aria seventy percent of the universe is dark matter,
black holes. What say we get sucked into one
and just before leaving our holographic image on its mouth
let's slow dance cheek to cheek on its surface,
toe to toe with our doppelgangers on the other side.
At music's end we'll slip through the hole,
faster than light, past our twins madly blowing kisses,
hoping Mr. Feynman wasn't jesting.

Come on, let's give those neutrinos a charge
and have at it after we dance the body electric
and just before we plunge into the unknown,
moan with the muon, gyrate with gravity's strings and loops,
finally permeate vast thicknesses without interaction
and wallow in the leftovers of creation.
Even if the libretto is bogus, it's the best sex we ever had.

*Lois Marie Harrod*

## Darkness, the Last Clown

Charles Wright

Darkness finally got his act together,
laid out his costume, the shimmering coat
that goes from bruise to black,
the sequined shoes, the make-up, he's got it right,

the lipstick smeared to indigo,
and a big fat kiss for you, the fat lady
in the front row, so much preparation
for the finale. You don't know if you should smirk

at his shenanigans or cry into your handkerchief,
you've tried so hard to smile and you still can't
talk through your teeth, but on with the dark
and his dummy, that white-faced moon.

On with the show. And what will you do
when attacked by his prattling prankster?
How long will you keep the balls aloft?
You know the sun is a juggler too.

## A January Night Like Chocolate

Nights like this
I want to throw
a suitcase in the car
a bag of sandwiches
a thermos, tapes
and just light out
heading west
on unmarked roads—
toss out the map!
we'll let old instincts lead us,
you and me and *Nuits d'Été,*
the full moon pearled
behind silkscreen, and
syrup-smooth
we'll top the mountains
pour onto the plains
(the skydome thin and clear
as Minnesota coffee) where
silver rivers run
crosshatched like snakes
alongside darkened cities
and all-night cafes
the juke box plays
*The New World,*
we'll pass up motels
—the Sleepy Hollow,
Heartland, Lucky Nugget—
hearts too light for sleep
bubbling like Dr. Pepper
through badlands, hulking buttes

*das Lied von der Erde*
and we'll ride
long curving canyons
red sand walls washed
to oystershell, and still
the frontier keeps on
spreading wide for us
(arriving everywhere
before the sun)
just us, the car,
the asking road,
our own lights carving
orbits through the dark.

*Juditha Dowd*

## *August 6, 1945 (Dresden)*

burnt wood and lead on wooden panels
Matthew Day Jackson, 2010

Confronted with the charred nubs of a ruined city,
the unrecognizable shops and dwellings viewed as from
the air, I remember that Heinrich Schütz lived there,
composing motets in another war, three centuries before.
*Warum toben die Heiden*—why do the pagans rage?
After Allied bombs laid bare the wooden beams, their
fire fell like rain. No doorway spared, no window.
Somewhere on this melted map his *Frauenkirche* fell,
its walls sucked down upon the organ, the *kappelmeister's*
tomb. A trunk forgotten in a back-street attic delivered
his secular works to flame. Music may still haunt this grid,
but all is silence, our eyes a desecration to the absence
we invade.

## No Breath, No Smut

i.

Capturing Henry Moore we call it
scrambling onto the base to stretch
long limbs, thrusting out a stomach
just where the donut hole was carved
from the granite, pretending our bodies
are encased in body stockings,
a Victorian *pose plastique* postcard
off-color, slightly out of focus,
nipples brushed away.

ii.

*Tableau vivante,* an image brought
to life, even though the actor
does not speak or move during
the ninety seconds on view,
the flutter of an eyelash allowed
yet no pause to heave or sigh;
a patch of skin is left untouched
by bronze paint or marbled white
to leave essential pores exposed.

iii.

*Photomontage,* an effect once
achieved with scissors, the head
of a woman fixed upon the body
of another, the resulting nude

retrieved in trepidation from
the camera store, manipulation
now done in a photo shop,
digital implies fingers,
the return key says enter.

*Maxine Susman*

## Self-Portrait, Provincelands

*Light*
*is most important,* he says,
*focus is least.*

I'm good at composition, find what I want
and take it,
I'm sometimes patient and lucky. I slip off
the beaten path.

> Full-tide at dawn, beach with thunderheads, marsh
> oozing to half-tide, fiddler crabs hefting their tools.

*Put something*, he says, *up close.*
*A few blades of grass can render scale.*
*Look for a pathway leading in, a flow*
*pulling you inside what you see—*

> path of moonlight, trail through dune,
> sun limbering the acrobat pitch pines.

(That's my dog, romping on the sand half-way to water's edge,
she's scared of water.)

*Don't put your subject in the center,*
*keep it off-kilter, give it pique, tilt,*
*give it a kick,*

*defeat expectation.*
As we learn is bound to happen.

I'm pretty good at perspective—
long view, close-up, odd angle,
zoom or telephoto—
        lean in, squat, climb, wait—

        sun-slants through slats of snow fence,
        a piping plover skittering by the wrack—

What of light?
I don't know how my camera captures it,
aperture, shutter speed,
I only know to capture what I see—
sunset, waves, gulls, all the clichés without
reflection—

and focus?
Also tied to luck,
luck and adjustment yoked to perspective,
which I say I'm good at.
        But to *stay* in focus—

as one instant crashes on another,
one breaker washing in
is blown
to a ghost of white scarf, outcry of foam?

        I'm learning adjustments,
light calibrated through a shifting lens.

He says, *find your places
and know them well. Return over and over.
They're never the same, an hour transforms them.*

We hike to Race Point Light, late August a half hour
before sunset, to catch just the right limpid bronze
as it shafts across salt hay and sculpted mud.

*Come back*, he says, *some day
in morning snow.*

*Lois Marie Harrod*

from *Nightmares of the Minor Poet*

The library room appears empty
except for stacks of metal chairs. No one there
to help. The poet dissembles the racks
into rows. Her black pants and turtleneck
collect dust and hair. She notices the custodian
uses this room to store toilet mops.
The facilitator arrives, egg yolk
in his beard. He disapproves
of her configuration, snarls, turns the chairs
the other way. There is no podium.
Four disheveled graybeards bumble in.
Each carries a three-ring chaos of scribbles.
The facilitator says, "This poet needs no introduction"
and does not introduce her. During her first poem
about the rusty sedan in the Quick Chek parking lot,
several high school kids enter–then a homeless,
he must be homeless, man with electric hair.
The room begins to smell like a urinal.
The poet reads her poem about over-watering petunias
while the students trade wads of verse
in the back row. They seem to have a bottle
of gin, but do not offer her a swig.

## They're Taking Your Music

I okayed Coltrane, Sun Ra, Mahler, Andean bombo and
those big guitars you said were made from shells of—what?—
armadillos. There go Dylan, Ringo and his pals, supreme
Diana, Bach and Bird, cloud chamber bowls of Harry Partch's
"Petals Fell on Petaluma."
Three thousand discs stopped spinning when you died.

Music takes strange turns. I was the player, you the listener.
But you heard more and deeper. It was always playing in your
mind.

                                Front door's
propped open, letting in the February cold, cat's under the
comforter. And I shiver. Two men from your favorite store
descend our crazy stairwell with its endless horizontal crack
that won't spackle. Some nights I still dream the second floor,
all yours, caves in, splits off, comes crashing down on my
head. How many tons of vinyl?

                           The movers stagger
under all this pent-up sound. I want to grab a disc and set it
playing, harsh or sweet. Hold back the tides of empty.

*Eloise Bruce*

# Alchemy in the Forest of Drawn Metal

after Robert Lobe's *Woodbury Quarry* (with Kathleen Gilje), an
98 x 96 x 24.5 inch oil on linen

air + lava  =  stone
stone + fire = metal

trees and rocks dressed in metal
drawn with the strokes of a hammer

in a dust of snow on stone,
he taps once and again

sound + metal = wind
hammer = metal + wood

insistently pounding
every rough surface

into another likeness of God
his alchemy insists she

make each stroke of the hammer
into the caresses of her brush

oily shadow and light on linen
trees + rocks = landscape

millions of grays embrace
transformed by the square root

of the hammer and the brush
which yields a pen

a pen x words = a poem
nesting in the forest of drawn metal

## Noteworthy

I've been falling in love
with things lately:
       the ball at the tip
       of my fountain pen,
       a key in my front door
       right before the click of the turn,
       the *s* sound at the end
       of a few extra pints of Guinness

I thought nothing of it
until I fell for the opening note
of hallelujah, and the note
started loving me back—
with promises to get me home
when monsoon nights feel endless
and the narrow road beyond
my bedroom window dwindles
to a footpath so slick, even snakes
shudder at the mere mention
of its name: Road

Since then, I've been singing
the *Hallelujah Chorus*
for the sake of that note

I have become the little girl who
has finally mastered the alphabet song
and is compelled to sprinkle it
into objects and available ears,

willing to crawl over bowls
of her favourite ice cream
to touch the edge of a new word

She's everything a little girl ought to be,
with sinews pulsating for all the joys
she finds in stories and fresh words,
and she salivates for the day
when she could go from singing *abcdefg*
into scenes and things raining down on a page

Maybe she'll even spell *hallelujah* one day

# Contained

after *The Old Lacemaker* by Nicholas Maes

Only your hands break the stillness,
plying the bobbins. Cross and twist,
hundreds of times, cross and twist,

nimbly as plucking a virginal
or a hen, you braid one complicated thing

in a pricked design with many strands.
Your scissors dangle on a cord.
Right hand works the pins, left hand the threads.

A room of earthenware and wood:
pitcher, jug, bundled round of kindling

in a wide-lipped jar, twigs bound in a whisk,
basket of eggs on the wall above your head.
You, recessed into a corner,

bleached points of your cap and collar,
the heavy apron folds, give enough white

to see the pillow on your knees. Spectacles
help you focus dimming eyes on the pattern
at your lap, while people four deep

crowd close and shuffle past your frame—
Once I saw an old woman, her humped spine

high as a backpack, ride a tricycle
down a bike path in Florida, her face
under a sunhat creased like yours from light.

Does every woman expect to end
with some task she manages herself

while couples and children pedal past?
In the year between husbands
I lived among my pots and shelves,

I would come home—it was enough—
in early dusk, to soup and bread.

You put aside your work and cross the tiles
to start the kindling, stir an egg, pour milk,
then take the lace into your lap again.

# Caryatids

The nut-tree sisterhood, what better name
for a row of crazy women, wearing hats
of entablature, pushing down their skirts
on a breezy porch, or frozen pilaster-flat
against a supporting wall,

sometimes forming the base of a table,
or candlesticks, standing as rigid
as a portmanteau, but no one available
to carry their cloaks,

one of them stolen by Lord Elgin,
the remaining five holding their poses
as if she were still with them, weight
shifted, *contrapposto*, three on
the right leg, three on the left,

and after more than a hundred years
of finger-pointing and posturing,
the girls themselves remind everyone
they are not slaves but merely brawny,
and comely,

coming from the same hometown as Helen,
a village of walnut trees, *Karyae*—hence
their name—where the nut women
placed baskets of live reeds
on their heads and danced.

Knowing/Not Knowing

*Lois Marie Harrod*

## The Woman Who Lost Her Heart

At first she didn't realize it was missing, her heart,
and then she panicked, searched the usual places—
windowsill, magazines, the top of the dresser with her rings.

Maybe she had wrapped it up with the linen
when she changed the bed or maybe it had fallen out of her chest
when she had opened the door to grab the mail.

She began again methodically, retracing her steps
through her rooms—the closet where she tossed her shoes
and the bathtub where she found her hair. Where was it?

She didn't know anyone who could steal her heart away.
Her friends told her not to worry, go on with life, they said.
A cousin mentioned that her spleen had been gone for a year

before her daughter found it in the library lost-and-found.
An old schoolmate discovered her spine in the glove compartment
after her husband had that terrible crash on Route 95.

Don't worry, said her therapist, hearts have a way of coming back.
But the woman's chest felt empty as it had
when her diamond had come loose in the dish water

and drifted down the drain. At night she woke suddenly,
like a woman electro-shocked back to life. For a moment
her heart seemed to have returned, to be trembling inside her,

but when she felt her pulse, nothing . . . nothing there.

## Paroxysms

Each week it got better, the words I brought him
from art class, *sfumato,* I said, and our lips
tried to do it right but we were laughing so hard,
holding our sides, *no wait,* I said, *morbidezza,*
never had so much fun with a boy, kissing
and studying Italian Mannerists, you know,

those twenty-somethings sitting around a table
sick of the Renaissance and Raphael, Madonna
of the cardinal and Madonna of the goldfinch,
how the sweetness unnerved them.
They wanted to paint elongated necks
and twisted limbs, distortion, smokiness
under the eyes, morbidity. All winter we were
kissing and not sure why everything was so funny.

Spring brought the Northern Renaissance,
Rogier van der Weyden and the Hospice de Beaune.
I didn't know my boy was gay, perhaps he didn't either.
He sent me a letter and a plant from the florist.
No more upheaval. No more paroxysms of laughter.
I always considered him the most courtly of lovers.

## Eve's Daughter

She craved to make—
who? She didn't even know,

conceived of me within, alone,

I'm a filament of her mind
as she is of yours—
don't deny the possibility,

though not in the Book I'm real
as Eve, as anyone
who isn't.

*Daughter* in her image,
not god man snake    the boys she bore
but someone with her cycles, circles,
her own way of power.

Ours,

women and young girls
who gave birth to the begats.
       Did you think only what's written remains?

While we lived we had names.

My brothers, the simple son and wicked son—
one killed, one fled—
while I, the wise child, stayed.

The rib's a pliant bone.

She kept me secret,
she'd learned from her mistake,
kept me from Adam, kept secrets from me
*for my own good*, she said
so how could I know her?

*Cleave*, the Book tells you—
meaning *cling to*, meaning *to split apart*.

I left her. How I miss her.

Other daughters sprang from somewhere
for the sons of men to marry.
Cain—did he tell the wife he took
of the brother he'd killed?

Sometimes I occur to you
(don't I?)

## Confessions to a Birth Mother

I threw so many rocks into our pond in the back yard
I may have made a small Bermuda Triangle there,
and I'm sorry for all the hours I spent doing that

Sorry, too, for pretending each rock I tried to drown
was you. Sorry for making some skim across the surface
so I could see how unsteadiness has its own beautiful dance

Sorry for not taking you seriously when you came to our
        house
groaning because something was wrong with you
(something was always wrong with you).
this time, you said, neuralgia made you bandage your face

You looked like Lazarus, but he used to be dead
and I couldn't find your reason to remind me of his story
At only eight or nine, what did I know of the difference
between games and tricks?

Like our secret game every time you convinced Mommy
to let you take me to the market where one
after another man would forget what he was
supposed to be buying and crash-land
onto your brown-sugar beauty. I used to love how it felt
to win when you whispered to me: *Tell him*
*today is your birthday,* and each in his turn
would give me money, usually $5.00, which I gave to you

Do you know you used to make me feel like I was born a
        spectator?
I watched you like a favorite student watches her teacher
and I learned steadily what not to be when I grew up
I suppose that makes you a good instructor

The truth is, this last pebble I toss into the pond today
is not you, and the skimming is not you. You are
the fleeting spaces each pebble makes across the surface
of the water. I am the ripple moving away from space and
        water

As I make it to the bank, I can say I came from pebble and
        space
Instead, I'm saying: I came from whatever a ripple is
before it is a ripple.

## At the Swimming Hole We Consider Female Body Image

?

Why did women do that to themselves, asks my middle
        granddaughter,
the ten-year-old. Her class is studying China. Why do *you*
        think,
I want to know. On bound feet we go, imagining the painful
        steps.
Then on through wasp waist and Botox, with a pause at
        anorexia.
Yes, they know a girl.

!

*I* eat, says the youngest—seven—shedding her jeans.
Yeah, but only sugar! scoffs the eldest. The four of us stare
        down
into the creek, regard our wavy reflections.

$

. . . but not "new" Barbie insists the youngest. *She* looks real.
I describe how an artist once extended "original" Barbie to
        person size.
She was nine feet tall and weighed one hundred and twenty,
doubled over by her boobs.

< >

The twelve-year-old titters in her new bra.

The middle girl, a gymnast, brings up exercise—what's
        excessive?
We dive into a whirlpool that's claimed a number of their
        friends.
Sometimes they can't stop, I say.

&

Oh, says the eldest, slowly meeting my eyes. You mean . . .
        like Aunt Kay.

# Five Ways to Grieve: Outline for an Instruction Manual

A. Simple version
    1. Get a dog
    2. Outlive your dog

B. Long-term version
    1. Bear a child
    2. Adore the kid's fingers and the indent at the back of the neck
    3. Watch your child grow up to be unhappy

C. International version
    1. Listen to the news
    2. Listen to the news again tomorrow
    3. Etc.

D. Sacred version
    1. Beg the sky gods to prove they exist
    2. Settle for earth

E. Deathbed version
    1.

    (There are no instructions)

    .

## Cento of Regret

All I desired was to change it back
the way it was, divert the river
separating us, narrow the rippling
circles of pain, in the gray light
of clouds and broken glass.

Water, simply flowing down
the hills, a perfect line of white
over the marker stones and rocks
paints all my longing,
all my fears. And I pretend

I could be you, swept up
in feathers I inherited from doves,
ignoring what is broken, could be broken,
like light through tinted glass.
Your hand is full of bones.

I'm standing on a frozen pond,
staring as if there's something to be seen
down there. Snow melts from stone,
where moss and fern outline my ignorance.
I am still sore from climbing stone walls
under the cover of hand-shaped leaves
heavy with blood. I have been made

a stranger in my home. I want
words from your dying tongue
stained like a fingerprint on glass,

all in bright clouds and clusters,
constellations of fireflies, I want
the slowness of moonlight feeling its way
around our darkened house.

I want magic, an unweeping willow,
drifting faces of the moon
singing to Earth. If there is no fog
on the night you come home, I will know
what god shines down on us.

## Motley Fool

after Bosch's *The Extraction of the Stone of Madness*, 1494

If only it were so simple:
trepanation, that ancient form
of ice fishing into the skull
to pluck the fish of madness,
render the patient whole

Our painter wants us to believe
the excess resides in a flower bulb
rather than a stone, much like his
later compatriots, tulipmania pulsing
in them like flowered avarice

The Tarot Card Fool carries
a flower to show his appreciation
of beauty, and not to make
it all too simple, his dog
represents carnal desire

Modern trepanation seeks
to relieve pressure in the cranium,
one false move and the patient
no longer knows what to call it,
the state of being a fool for love

## Lucid Dreaming

I tell myself we are in the car,
   driving over the crest of a hill—
that a man spent his life inventing the car.

And just in case we're wondering what we're doing here,
I say: We're here to invent the car. Here to pave the roads.
We are here to eat our macaroons,
     though I seem to be alone.

Then for a brief time I'm allowed
   to visit my grandmother's dining room,
     to see her mother's silver-plate
waiting to be polished as I go upstairs to bed.
And the others getting out their maps and newspapers
in the Art Deco light of the waning forties.

This is our way, I say, or want to. This explains the stars.
And because I'm driving and not a bit hungry,
I know I must still be dreaming.
I hear again those words spoken at the door of sleep—
*purloined* and *antimacassar*
and more we've so wickedly abandoned
   to make way for hijack and headset.

I know the voice. It is yours. *Bailiwick, perdition,*
   wandering down the hall.
     Didn't you mean them?

This is a reason why we should have been given sleep,
                                        and were.
And biscuits being buttered in the driveway,
        my brother dawdling his jar of jam.

Then here we go again, inventing the car.
Here, as we would be          as we are.

*Judy Rowe Michaels*

## You Know Those Nights When a Word Keeps Visiting?

This time it's *heft*— graffito you feel your

fingers loop repeatedly, on dream walls.

You half hear a whispered *h*, feel teeth bite lip, *f*,

tongue cross the *t*. *Heft* of newsprint, of eggplant, tumor,

heft of fashionable boot, of stolid owl in fork

of oak tree near the bedroom window, former heft

of desiccated bug under the stove, of time wasted, forgotten,

heft of the timeless, of clotted blood, of—O, hear them—

heft of cathedral tunes, of uphill and downhill, of cat's steely

calculation, heft of United War Veterans' brochure

(in thanks for old sweaters) quoting Lincoln,

*To care for him who shall have borne the battle,*

*his widow and his orphan*, heft of good rhythm everywhere

giving way to tomorrow's word, hear the swish

of its silky parachute, *husk*, try it,

                              heft of the husk of you.

## *Show Me How to Survive Under a Heating Vent*

Tom Sleigh

I could do it.
Could worship the moment
the hot air comes on
or late afternoons when sunlight slices in.
How sometimes a wind
sings through the metal wings of the vent.
I could be a creature of skin under fur
and the fur blowing slightly
when the heat comes on.

When the heat comes on
in my body between the bones
when the belly craves
without knowing what it craves
maybe it's the old rush of lilac
the smell of girlhood longing
when I first learned to sleep with a dog
me and my Irish setter
in our chaste single bed
where the dog went to bed first
and I curled around her
and she was my hot heart.
I remember the throbbing.

If I tried to explain this to my good husband
to whom I am precious
and incomprehensible

I would shiver under that heating vent
and I would be lonesome
and without fur.

*Eloise Bruce*

## Considering My Cruelties

\*

Question your perception if you think you see a stone
resting at the bottom of a stream
rushing through a tangle of shiny green trees.
The jungle floor is not littered with twigs
and  a carpet of soft fallen leaves,
and that is not a single pink orchid growing high in the canopy.

\*

Keep your eye on the mouth of the cave
where I depend on the artistry of shadow,
working my dark shape across the cold wet wall,
in a panorama of shimmering shades meant to resemble life.

\*

I have never killed a man after coitus
so do not mistake me for a mantis or a wild orchid.
I am a creature who camouflages
like a leaf mimic, a stick bug, a stone fish.
I can be as invisible as the clearest jelly fish.

\*

My prisoners have never seen me as they gaze forward,
chained so their necks are fixed. They only perceive my outline,
the travesty, the iota, and think I am real.
My prisoners are also puppeteers, camouflaged
and like lyrebirds their voices
scream like chainsaws and sirens.


\*

I am simultaneously chained
and gazing at the shapes and shadows crossing a cave wall.
The flicker of the fire, like the false beacon
of a firefly luring me to mate
but coming to steal my life's blood.


\*

Remember, that is an insect, not a pink orchid
growing high in the canopy soaring above
the false carpet of twigs and dead leaves.


\*

A fish lies hidden disguised as a stone,
the stream rushes through his scales
and the water distorts the reflections
of the rising tangle of shadow upon shadow.

## *Nowadays*

And is that everything
since you? *Since* meaning
*posthumous.*
               Here melancholy's
interrupted by brief flirt
with dictionary: originally
*postumas*, no hint
of burial in living earth.

Dicking around again with
missing you, post this and that—
coital, colonial, menopausal,
Mesozoic, coitus interruptus. . . .
Nowadays sex is catch-all for
almost anything, god, war,
cupcakes, abs and apps, the boat
is listing.
               Poet Gilbert, Jack, said
"the erotic matters not as pleasure
but a way to get to something
darker." He's restless
when people laugh a lot,
he prefers Greek fishermen,
who "do not play on the beach."
Is it so wrong to heft
an inflatable ball, twirl it
on a finger, think circus seals?

Wasn't sex mostly a three-ring
circus—three or more, given
the presence of memory, fantasy,
irony, flattery, usury, syzygy—
that's sun, moon, earth aligned,
and then there's the all-but-impossible
synergy, two becoming a
greater third,
                    yes, *Nowadays*
is everything since that.

*Gretna Wilkinson*

## The Last Time I was Surprised

i stumbled upon a small rose
that had slipped outside a painting.

the frame looked straight ahead,
its back against the wall.

it was the morning of my wedding, and two
village elders were on their way to *bathe the bride.*

i felt like the rose with its roots exposed, and close
to knowing permanent shame for all roots,

had it not been for the stem. so stately.
so bereft of a single thorn to right it again

when the winds show up. that's the last time
i was surprised by anything, for a rosebush

that has lost its thornability is like rice cooked
without water, or salt that tastes like sugar.

as the bathers and their bucket of water approached

our outside bathroom, I tried to imagine who had

done this deed to a rose, still so obviously young

for even the smallest vase. i concluded that

that if an artist can do this to a painting,

then I can believe the following:

    Roses are like raindrops.

    Even if it falls sideways,

    rain will always leave you wet.

    Despite the unnatural position,

    Dear Artist, you can never

    strip a rose of its rosiness.

          Why?

    Because a rose is an idea

    Because a rose is an idea.

Critters like Us

*Maxine Susman*

## Discovering Mildew in the Baby Clothes

Pungent odor, not entirely
awful. Marigolds, wilted cabbage,
smells you're not supposed to like—

I spread old baby things on the deck
in sunshine all day, red, yellow, blue,
primary ones I had to keep—

to remember how small, my babies,
swallowed by soft casings, and
how fully they gave shape to my enfoldings,

just my favorites, later they had theirs:
sleep-sacs then pajamas, onesies then Oshkosh,
a hoodie, size of a hankie, its two little snaps,

a kind of hoarding. More than I needed
to save, like many memories,
forgotten until they spilled out,

the caboodle tumbling from the old suitcase,
bundled in mold,
and somehow I like thinking that

although they may be past redeeming
they didn't just molder in the dark
but came jolting back into daylight,

rank as cheese, as memory
double-takes you with reproach,
what you manage fine without

until you open and recall little things
smelling to heaven, spread like blossoms
in a circle at your feet.

## Miss Hilda Has Joined Our Staff

Miss Hilda takes her scalpel
draws a line across your thigh

slow as a leaf-cutter ant

Blood-ferns bloom
along the slice

She severs a small artery

bathes lazy fingers in the drops
that puddle on the table top

You will not whimper, cry aloud

With threadlike tweezers she plucks out
the capillaries, fine blue feathers

Oh, the white-veined leaves

white lizards, tiny sucking feet
the silhouette of tulip trees

against a paling sky

blue   ash-gray
white

## My Dog Lily

I call her *Madame Pre-rinse*
because she licks plates
and is a dog of gourmet tastes
fond of expensive balsamic
and once just once
I treated her to octopus and yes
that was a hit and I could go on
with small semi-witty remarks
about the dog or how these hills
are greening like green felt
on a billiard table but with the hills
too lumpy for billiards
and while you wait for gourmet dog
to trot back into the poem
you are beginning to daydream
about something else
like the octopus you ate in Spain
or a call you're waiting for
or why I titled this poem My Dog Lily
and then changed subjects.

Please don't feel bad if you wander
which would be just fine
because I want you to think about
whatever you think about
when you're not thinking about
something else
and for some people it's sex

which might be nice I know
I don't think about sex nearly
enough these days
I think about chores unfinished
or chores unstarted
I think about who has cancer
or how much my eyes itch
and I notice everything blooming
too early this Spring
and say *global climate change*
or *wow those magnolias*
and tomorrow the fallen petals
like a storm of pink snow
will frost the unmown lawn.

Here I could jump back to my dog
who as you know by now
is really named *Lily* not *Pre-rinse*
and discuss recipes
for keeping octopus tender
or instead I could ask you
where your mind has traveled
since you last tuned in
to my disconnected mumblings
and you may have been
someplace amazing or secret
or maybe just wishing
for a glass of decent red wine
and I could uncork it
and pour two generous glasses
so you and I could sit here

with the dog sprawled on the floor
and clink wine glasses
and say what we've been unwilling
to speak out loud
like *Come on is this really a poem*
or *I kiss my dog on her lips.*

*Eloise Bruce*

## Feasting on the Bread of Fairies

*Roasted, boiled, or raw, silverweed's rootstock has been consumed as food by the Native Americans, Chinese, and Europeans for centuries. Silverweed rootstock has kept people alive when nothing else was available to eat.* Traditional Medicine

Roots of silverweed,
in the time when people were new
and the ice retreated from the land,
you fed the fairies,
and your leaves were brushed by their wings.

      Bounty in time of famine,
      footing tendrils of filigree,
      vibrating like strings. Calling out in starvation time.
      Tasting like words in the mouth,
      a mouth that drank the blood of the old language.

Pleasured by the wings that caressed you
with an appetite for the ephemeral,
kin of roses and breath to the hungry,
remembering the wild cattle
who would not suffer our human touch,
I call out to you from the future.

*Gretna Wilkinson*

## Farmhands

There was a time
when playing house meant:
the three of us getting help from our mother
to make a coal fire under our house
and try our hands at cooking

But her larder could never rival
the excitement we would get
from running past our own farm
to pilfer enough goods from our neighbours' farms
to half-fill the antique iron pot
now simmering over the red-hot coals

It didn't matter that the stolen plantains
were too young to taste like any thing
or the eggs we had pinched
from under one of their hens
were clearly on their way to chickenhood

After all, this was summer
and our hormones were spreading
like slow-rising yeast
on my sister's chest
and my brother's armpits

We were 10, 11, and 12 year olds,
and we probably knew
that time had begun to chase us

What if in our running,
we ended up in places
where the northeast trade winds
could not reach? What if
my sister picked her own
physically abusive mate? What if
I would lack my sister's courage
To choose my own abuser
and end up condemmed to one
who knew how to pummel
my mental and emotional muscles? What if?

So we must ignore our own farm for now

It will always be there
willing to strip us of fun
with its constant closeness
and predictable giftings

*Juditha Dowd*

# Hooks

Our mother loathed those shimmering trout, refused
to gut the smelly things or scrub the pan.

So he did it himself—fried them up for breakfast,
whistling the day into what could pass for happiness.

I'd side with her if it came to that, though it seldom would—
her resentment plain in the whir of the kitchen fan.

Yet she'd stay in motels at Cape Hatteras, where he went
to fish for blues—sit on a bed and watch the rain,

her youngest boy with nothing to do but stare at the TV
or beg her to play just one more game of Go Fish.

Decades later, not far from there, I caught a mackerel
with his pole, got up with the dawn to go after more.

I like to think that might have pleased my father, unless
he'd scorn the wasted bait, fish too small to bother.

That night I phoned the brother we tease, ever
his father's son—a need to hear familiar laughter.

*You*, fish? he said, and we talked for over an hour.
By fine bewilderments we knew them, have come to know

ourselves. And our children—what of them? Already
they claim bemusement at the tangled ways of love.

*Lois Marie Harrod*

## The Spineless

No use telling
the jellyfish
to stand up
for herself
or the footless
slug to stand
his ground.
Most amoebae
are wobbly
as curdled milk
and even
the centipede
for all his feet
doesn't know
which one
to put down.
White feathers
quiver
the slightest breeze,
and backboneless
crabs sidle off.
So don't expect
piling or prop.

90% of us
have been spineless
this 3.7 billion-year
epoch.

*Eloise Bruce*

## Old Dog

Breathe, she does and her breath
smells of decay and the sea
If only the dry bones had been wet
when God breathed on them

Smells of decay and the sea
her breath is the wind rising
when God breathed on them
She rests in the crook of my arm

her breath is the wind rising
If only the dry bones had been wet
She rests in the crook of my arm
breathe, she does and her breath...

## Fiddler Crabs

We drop, the dog and I, from woods to marsh,
mid-tide, intruding on their busy village life,
crowds taking sun in front of doorway holes—
we send them scurrying, waves of creatures
rushing to their tunnels, polka dots in mudsand
running on many claws, little bellybodies
sideways, the females skittering their ballet,
males brandishing swollen claws like clubs
in threat since threatened. We Gullivers discover
more than it seems we should, their foraging hours
when tide uncovers the flux they surface for,
scudding through strands of cord grass and salt hay.
We climb back to the pitch pines, leave to them
the briny scent of slowly filling cove.

# Private Vow

*Vermont Studio Center*

Wasps come from somewhere every night.
Mornings my floor is littered
with dark shapes, like daggers laid
for some unfeeling hand to hurl.

It snows now every day,
some days hard, all day, and blowing,
others, the air is full of flakes
that never touch the ground.

These signs make me restless.
What if the year should turn without my noticing?
If I should stay away too long,
the road deny me the way back?

I will bring bones, the long bone and the skull,
I will arrange them carefully,
eye socket, jaw, a rib.
I will ask a blessing.

The roads that brought me to this place
were narrow, wound around the mountains
and long grey lakes. I thought a map.
To go back, I should only have to turn it over.

If everything goes right, when I return
I will keep house, fastidious.
I will not let the fires go out.
I will not forget to render thanks.

## Worst Fire Season on Record

All day the doves
hid among leaves,
jaunty quail
failed to parade.
Even the finches
ditched the feeder.
Not a sparrow
pecked at the ground.

The valley stayed narrow
and smoke-yellow.
All the mountains
didn't exist.
Everyone in town
ate smoke for supper.
The quarter moon
shone dim orange.

Even the dog
sagged on the couch,
her hipbones
defeated.
Don't tell me
this is the hottest year on record.
I already know
this is the driest year on record.

I hesitate to think
how this world will end:

the small lizards
crouched among rocks,
their whole elastic bodies
breathing out, breathing in.

## Ice Fishing

There in the acrid air
and hush of the tiny house
tangy with birch smoke

the only light rose
through water glowing the green
of Breughel's winter sky.

Staring down
the sharp-etched hole
your life condensed

thin and tense
as the line that vanished
underneath your feet

the stiff translucent skin
of water all
that held you

from falling
through the moment
to where fish hung

suspended in the glow
and you half wanted
to follow.

*Sharon Olson*

## The Miraculous Draught of Fishes

after Raphael

*Keep 'em coming,* the Pilot said, as would-be customers
cheered expectantly on the distant shore. Fish spilled
over the edge of the boats, enough for everyone—even
the cranes applauded, open-mouthed—as the disciples
reached down for the nets, sun on their muscled arms.

A moment of reflection, that is what we see, pointing
figures mirrored in the water, a leg here, a blue garment
there, the white skirts of Jesus taking on a tinge of red
under the surface, as if warmth and reassurance colored
the entire scene. We wait at the table with hands clasped.

And I dreamed this, a few days after my father died:
he and I on the beach together, anxiously rushing about
to rustle up enough boats, and it seemed we were letting
fish down into the water, instead of the other way around,
but it did not matter, these were my father's arms.

A miraculous draught they called it, a current of air,
the act of pulling a load, a portion of liquid, a gulp
or swallow, the amount inhaled in one breath,
the boat with its surprising cargo
drifting away.

*Judy Rowe Michaels*

## Poem with Swan

A swan walks into this bar,
here, in the poem we're writing,
you and I, my reader,

*mon frère, mon semblable.*
It's swanning around, cadging
drinks, it knows what it wants—

that girl, what's-her-name, she's
in her swan period, and some
swans don't mind blood

on their whites, it could happen
right here, given we're all plugged
into our own music (mine's the old

jazz standards). "Plugged" you like,
you tell me to write "with a bullet,"
but it's so been-there-done-that

and no nuance, god help the *if*s and *but*'s.
No, gods are too busy
donning feathers, preening

so they can get the girl. Whose
only hope is the bullet she hasn't
got. You tell me

our poem's about guns.
I say our girl may soon need one
of those (closed) abortion

clinics. Let's erase that, you say,
but my eraser's worn down to the bone,
pencil's a souvenir wrapped in haiku,

*Autumn wind—like thoughts*
*in the mind of Issa*. Should we just
blow off this poem? No, you say,

we need to shoot the swan.

On Further Thought

*Eloise Bruce*

## Cold Day, Meditation on Electrons

My palms tickled by the seeds singing in my hand,
the song rises and floats in puffs,
the aroma of roasted peppers
landing on my tongue. A mouthful of raspy vibrations
to be gulped quickly, warming me against winter
when ice splinters and snow drifts.

*Judy Rowe Michaels*

# Living with cancer is like,

well, marriage? Different, of course,
and maybe John Donne could work this out,
as September mist rises off the lake,
drifts sideways toward the cove
to die in the shore's curved
arms.
　　　　　Seventeen years in dalliance
with cancer, marriage was forty-three.
Here Donne might do something clever with
numbers in relation to sex and death?
I'm more disposed to wonder how one loses
track of cancer/marriage while
it deepens its hold. This morning,
claw marks cross the beach,
pressed in too hard for coon or dog.

After pricks, scans, testing
and being tested, one can drift
months, through anniversaries,
maintenance drugs, the weekly
run for gas and peanut butter,
kisses, spats, kisses,
unrecognized shifts in allegiance,
in climate, habitat, taste buds,
but underlying all these a steady pulse
of self, obligation to self.

Somehow, one got off track.
Missed the signs. Cancer renews

its vows—in sickness or in health,
depending on one's viewpoint, snaps
on the wedlock, lays down the don't
and do, and with a jolt you're no longer
one but two.

## Lady Slippers

Years since we found them.
Though late now, worth a try.
The woods are boggy,
undergrowth taking over, it's easy

to get turned around and lost almost
within sight of the house.
Slow going. We follow faint traces
of the old trail to the stream,

find the very spot where a clump
of veiny-pink pouches hung then
from their delicate stems,
covered today with vivid thrusting ferns.

We wobble downstream—
the rocks ankle-twisters—
you maneuver your walking stick
to break the jolts and stumbles,

wincing when you misstep.
The stream widens a bit,
light shows where trees thin out
to sky above the lake,

we break onto the road
jubilant from woods—

you're spent, your back stabs
where the tumor kindles,

I go for the car and leave you
grinning at the bottom of the hill.

# In the Cathedral of *I Remember You*

You've left tokens everywhere,
littering the crypt,
rolled up against the pillars.
I wish I could refuse those gifts,

fares for a trip I can't afford.
I watched you take your ride,
rails sliding through the leather door.
That copper burning of the mind.

If only all fire sank to ash—
but your voice goes on, scorching
and secret as the faces
of God. Inside your church

I know without a bulletin
somebody is always dying.

*Juditha Dowd*

# Elegy from a Distance of Years

The second time, I fly all night
with my next-to-youngest brother
because I've made him come.
On the drive to Santa Rosa there's
nobody on the road. Most of the time
we seem airborne. It's three when we
arrive. Bathed in hospital twilight
our family spills over plastic chairs,
waiting for us in the waiting room—
their faces ashen, blasted. Can anyone
live in this air? Last week our father
was tethered, unable to speak but hopeful.
Just a scare. Now he knows he won't
make it, that if somehow he does the
respirator is forever.

      A paper scrap,
his shaky hand—he won't play for stakes
this low. I beg his silence please try.
No. His eyes go wild and he wrenches
his head from side to side. He understands
I have contacts, can ask for a different drug
or order Medevac, get him out of here.
That only I will oppose him.

                              While I mouth
the jargon of grief, he mimes a language
of dying till finally he relaxes, winks
at me, as if this were already done.
Then he hardly sees us so busy is he,
departing.

*Gretna Wilkinson*

# Journal: Day # 9 Since the Surgery

*(what she said)*

My Darling, it's tomorrow again.
The rains came twice this week,
for three days, then for two days

Last night I opened the windows
on the south side. The moon was
full of itself, and the okra trees
seemed cowed by its silence

I was wearing the night shirt I made you,
the one you always accused of leaving
a trail of light around me, and I believed you
every time and helped you wake up
on the sweet side of the bed the next morning

I stared at the okra and thought of your arm
hooked in mine as we walked amongst them
and discussed the price of the coming crop.

You said, *even okras should be sold
for their worth so they don't feel cheap*

Oh, and I arranged the furniture
the way you like:
> the lamp on the coffee table to your right
> as you walk into the drawing room,
> and the little doilies under the decanter
> and wine glasses

I washed, starched, ironed, and rehung
all of the curtains last week, and now
the living room looks like it will start
to come alive soon

I am fighting for approval
to bring running water upstairs
for the new sink you attached
outside the kitchen window

It's late, but I must tell you
one last thing: Without you, my bones
have sprung a leak. I think it's because
I can't rid myself of the feeling
that when they opened your heart,
they attacked mine.

So, mend quickly My Darling. Mend

*Lois Marie Harrod*

## *Pulvis et umbra sumus*

*We are but dust and shadow.* Horace, *The Odes*

My shadows have left me, she said,
the dust, so much diffuse light

from every direction, I can't remember
when I last saw a shade, my own,

tipping towards me here, there
leaning away in the sand.

My sister says I never come to see her
though I visit twice a year,

my friend always reluctant
to be anywhere I am on time—

so much diffuse light
reducing harsh shadow, glare

no lines, no blemishes—
I have tried so hard to be kind.

*Juditha Dowd*

## Downsizing

We've kept them alive as long as we can
the ancestors
Grandfather's Thanksgiving cactus
soon to be ninety years old
Great-grandma's hand-knit bed socks
that warmed the generations
when keeping windows open a crack
was what you did for your health

We'll still enjoy our oysters
but not on flow blue Minton plates
the Antiques Road Show estimates
would go for a couple of hundred apiece
assuming we wanted to sell
or considerably more for a perfect set
which they used to be
till the sons did the dishes one Christmas

We've watched their pictures fade
the ancestors framed on our walls
or waving from dilapidated boxes
that once held their sandals and pumps
What's to become of this flapper dress
someone once borrowed and tore
when I offer it to our daughters
who have so little room
What of all the photographs
they bequeath to ether and cloud

# That Day

Auden wrote about my brother,
the way no one saw his plane go down.
No image survives, no Kodachrome
or Brownie print, no news flash
or YouTube clip, no time machine
to take me back to April 13, 1953,
his 21st birthday, going up
in the plane he had so recently
purchased, and couldn't wait.
Someone standing alongside his car
at ocean's edge might have seen him
but looked away, and when he looked
back again the thing was gone,
and he didn't puzzle over how much time
had passed, or where a plane could have
disappeared, around the back
side of a cliff, for example,
like a page had turned and all
the words that came before
were gone, *tabula rasa,* not even
the remnants of something erased,
palimpsest, a clue, a morsel,
talisman, touchstone,
hand of my brother on my forehead
as I went to sleep.

## Cutting Clouds

The vapors, my father said when Mama complained
*corn meal for dinner*; we should thank God
we have mush to eat, let us pray. But Mama knew blood
was slicker than water and grew thick in winter
when it wasn't safe to go without hot soup.
Can't cut ice with a cold knife, she muttered.
We need bread. We need meat. Without,
she dressed us in flimsy fabric, smoothing one cloud
after another across the kitchen table to cut our clothes.
The turnips boiled furiously into an afternoon stupor
as she clipped out diaphanous frocks,
but we grew afraid when she fitted the murk to our chins
and trimmed against the jugular. It's true:
none of us went to Sunday School naked,
but we didn't see Mama face to face
with the kitchen so hazed and steamed.
The congregation thought her proud, but who else
made do with almost nothing? My smallest sister
got the hand-me-downs, the mist lifting, the gloom
burning off the hills, which may be why she now sees
through the smog darkly while the rest of us are dim
and have difficulty lifting up our eyes.

*Judy Rowe Michaels*

## Speaking to the Medical Students

We sit before them,
three old women
diagnosed late-stage,

come back from the dead—
almost—to tell our stories.
We pole our three boats

across the river of fire, river
of blood, of wailing, relive
years of hope and error, our own

and all our white-coat shamans',
pay tribute again:
ovaries, womb, hair, bone,

drugging the creature
that hid in us, only to feel him
wake and grow again.

This stale classroom air
is hard to breathe. . . .
But then a hand goes up,

another. We feel the tug—
their questions, drawing us
safely back to shore.

## The Two Cakes

We couldn't believe how easy it was,
the recipe from the newspaper said
to heat some white sugar in a pan,
watch it closely so it wouldn't burn,
and it would turn into a dark syrup
called burnt sugar, and some of it
would go into the cake, mixed with
real butter and cake flour, and some
of it would go into the icing, so sweet
I would chase it with iced cola when
I sat with my mother in the kitchen
after school, and it became a success
for her, a signature cake she would
produce for company, or just for us,
on Sundays, an exercise that helped her
forget the other cake she used to make,
the lemon-frosted angel food my older
brother loved, especially the one
she sent him on his twenty-first birthday,
for which he thanked her in a letter,
his last. She showed it to me recently,
then it was put away.

## His Eye

Somewhere where terrible things happen—
not here, though terrible things do happen—
but somewhere they happen more frequently
(and I read about this, I didn't see it first hand),
a boy was beaten so fiercely that one eyeball
fell out of his head, and he carried his own eye
safe in the palm of his hand over many miles
to the nearest doctor and begged the doctor
please to sew his eye back in its raw socket
but of course the doctor couldn't sew it back
(I suppose the optic nerve was severed and
who knows what all else) so that loose eye
was thrown out or buried, who knows which,
because that detail wasn't in the story I read,
but here's what I do know: forever afterward
the boy's hand, the hand that carried the eye,
was gifted with vision. If he touched a stone,
he knew the hidden inside color of that stone,
and when he grew up and touched a woman,
he knew, more fully than anyone else could,
all the untold dread that made her beautiful.

*Eloise Bruce*

## *Kairos*

The ancient Greeks had two words for time, *chronos* and *kairos*.
While the former refers to chronological or sequential time, the
latter signifies a time lapse, a moment of indeterminate time in
which everything happens.

In a cosmological minute Christ is born and so am I.
In the eons it takes God to draw one breath
the twelve horsemen of the apocalypse
brush past each other trillions of times
as they avoid collision with uncountable angels
dancing on the head of a pin.

What happens now causes changes
in what happened before.

I cannot hold the thought
that it is not yet now and no longer now,
as I continue on my journey
to my eternal destination. Time persists
in occurring to me like a river
flowing in one direction from one now-point to the next.

I wait for this and that and
am mostly unaware of my disconnection from my soul.
Souls do not live in the moment
but in some other framework that is not now.
When I sleep, my dreams are not now
and I am vaguely aware of my soul nesting in them.
*Kairos* is an otherworldly place
largely unchanged since the birth of the universe.

In God's time zone he still wraps time
unbounded around his little finger,
holds its fluidity on the tip of his tongue.
And there is no waiting, how could there be?

Beyond Ourselves

## Large-Billed Reed Warblers

*In the beginning, all the world was America.*
John Locke

Audubon was hunter as much as naturalist,
providing for his table and his art.
Yet it's right to say he loved the birds he drew
even as by the thousands they were sacrificed.
When late in life he sat for portraits
he complained his eyes were rendered as angry coals.
Perhaps the artists meant to show him avid,
a woodsman, hinting at the penniless years,
birds that disappeared before he captured them.

Today he'd fly to Afghanistan, searching
for a flock discovered in the Wakhan peaks,
a species feared extinct for nearly a century.
But today he'd press for catch and release,
wouldn't he, instead of guns a camera?
Now, when twenty warblers, olive-brown
and inconspicuous as wrens, are news—
and even his young America has squandered
what was once the world?

*Gretna Wilkinson*

## to be        young        gifted        & dead

*(for Tamir Rice-12, Michael Brown-18, Walter Scott-50, Tony
Robinson-19, Eric Crawford-22, Eric Garner-43, Tanisha
Anderson-37, Phillip White-32, and too many more)*

the after-school job that never got your application
social security income you won't retire to collect

the high school halls teeming with pretty girls
their fingerprints on lockers and the secrets they hold

the size nine sneakers you won't bug your parents to buy—
                these miss you

your sister screams at the empty swing swaying in her dreams
she reaches for you from the back of a police car—
                she's missing you

the cops-and-robbers game you wanted to play alone
the officer who joined the game saying, *Me Cop, Me Robber*

the grand jury convening a committee to form a committee
to select the committee that will discuss plans

to study the efficacy of hearing your case
at a future date to be determined by the Date Committee—
                they     well     they don't miss you

the angels at your birth who vowed to keep you safe
the God who prayed you would live long and remember
Him—

the angels, the God, the prayer
— they miss you missing them

*Whose fault is it if a bullet, a choke
hold, a broken taillight, or pepper
spray killed the kid? He walk in
front of it. Didn't he?*

*Lois Marie Harrod*

## *Like a Maelstrom with a Notch*

*Emily Dickinson*

And when the clothing factory collapsed
in Dhaka, Bangladesh, one young seamstress
was trapped in the Muslim prayer room
which also stored boxes of skirts and shawls,
shirts, sheers, socks and sequins,
and for those in need, a few prayer cloths
thrown over pipes and stretching to a strut or two.

And when that nineteen-year-old was rescued,
it was a miracle because we wanted to believe
that we too can survive, ignorant and inventive,
disregarding the adjacent, the close-by distant
dead, sucking air through shaky pipes, licking
the leaking rain, yes, washing our faces, knowing
whatever those gods of mercy had done to others
they had not yet done it to us. That miracle.

And of course, to keep sane, she did find things to do,
packed and unpacked the boxes of saris in her little room,
maybe the first she had ever had to herself,
changed her clothes repeatedly as teenagers do,
why not, hadn't she always wanted to try them on?–
so that after seventeen days when someone at last
heard her cry, she was wearing a radiant red scarf
around her neck, as if she had just tripped off a runway–
a scarf any one of us might buy for almost nothing.

116

# Mayflower Landing

Corn Hill, Cape Cod

*Monday, the 13ᵗʰ November [1620]....Our people went on shore to refresh themselves, and our women to [do the] wash, as they had great need....* Mourt's Relation

### The Men

The ship pulls as close as sand flats allow.
Men row to shore with flaccid muscles,
hungry mouths full of God.

Some of them march off to lay their claim—
to climb, to dig, to shout their find:
a huge iron kettle, a basket "cunningly made"

and full of corn. Whose food, winter coming?
Salvation theirs by virtue
of discovery. First theft in a new place,

first of many trespasses.


### The Women

Released from crammed berths
and pitching planks,
nausea, tedium, wailing, suckling,
a hold's worth of smells and stains,
the women do the wash.

They spread to the sun
the linen of rough passage
to bleach on widening sand.

# In the Ruins of Dholavira

—a city in northern India that flourished c. 3000 BC

I have spent so long over this hollowed grinding stone
that my hair is turning to millet.

In my small house which touches my neighbor's house
which touches her neighbor's house

I have been grinding for five thousand years.
When I began, this town was rich

and I could see down to the harbor where dhows came in
from far coasts. Now the sea is salt white desert.

When the breeze blows between gateless stone pillars, dust
smells like sweat from my loose blouse.

The interlocking reservoirs are empty and there is no water
in the channels. The stone walls

my husband once helped pry into place still stand square
and I am still pregnant.

*Lois Marie Harrod*

## The Legend of the Straw Heart

In our village there was a man who seemed to be made like the rest of us, but the witch doctors said he had been born with a heart three times bigger than our own. Consequently, he could run farther and swim longer than any of us and each wanted him in his hunting group. When he let us put our ears to his chest, as he sometimes did if we stopped to warm ourselves in the sun, we could hear the blood slurping and sucking as through a thousand reeds, each a little sluice to flume his blood. We wondered how this could be, but we did not begrudge him his big heart because he was always generous, lifting us to his back if we had strayed too far from our huts. We said he was like his mother who could swim the coldest waters and divided her fish evenly among us. So we were startled when he died, and the witch doctor lifted out his heart, as is our custom upon death, and revealed it was straw. How could we not pull at the pieces to see who got the long and the short of it?

*Sharon Olson*

# The Sacred and the Profane

*The voice between her lips,*
*and the viol between her legs*
Thomas Middleton

1.
Arranged within white-gated pews
we partake of an evening's refreshment,
viola da gamba, a singular instrument
that cannot stand but must be grasped
between the legs and lightly bowed.

2.
The street crowd oohed and aahed
as the breakdancers dove under
an arc of women's legs, and
these women, willing, widened
their stance to help the buskers pass.

3.
We look for an opening, too,
a hinge that beckons us, the back
and forth movement of a song,
which plays so deep inside
we cannot even stand, can only gasp.

## Mazaruni River, Guyana

It's Saturday morning, and the sun
has not yet made its way through
the leaves blanketing the river

The monsoon has left the Mazaruni
stuffed with bowed trees and
crisscrossed branches. I am 16,
floating in a small canoe

I dip my girl-size paddle one side or the other
just enough to skirt around the branches
and occasional trunk

Soft mud, smelling fresh from a new spring cycle
hugs the bank. Even the lone bird high up in a tree
sings its awareness, with the nearby waterfall
for a back-up chorus. I begin to believe
this moment is nature's way
of listening to her own prayer.

Here, stillness and sound are homogenized
And a mysterious fragrance wakes up
inside of me.

An hour—maybe two months—maybe a year later,
I return home. I tie the canoe to the landing
but carry the jungle into the house

## Spring Rain

He's forty. His mother dies.
Home to Iga-Ueno to wind up her affairs,
he stumbles upon—let him tell it:

> *At my native village*
> *I wept over my umbilical cord*
> *first rain of spring*

By then he had become Bashō,
restless, lonely haiku master shifting
from one rustic hut to another,
making his first journey to the interior.

Was it a lashing rain
or gentle?

Soon he would register the frog's leap and water sounds
together:
*furu ike ya / kawazu tobikomu / mizu no oto*

It takes translation and more
to move under the ruffled water
into simultaneities
of sound and act, near and far,
before and now. To weep
for a stranger and discover
he is not.
       It would be like
holding in your palm

a shriveled, frail piece of you
and your dead mother.
Bubbles rising to the surface
of the old pond.

Perhaps he will
bury the cord in her grave,
proof to a god
of her motherhood.

## Recapture the Glory

Frost on this morning's window
makes a map, and it's the map
of my old neighborhood: there's
Mickey's house, and Mary Beth's,
and Tommy Wallen's. Cold
is a smell from long ago,
when winter had no shore,
an ocean of ice you'd never get across.

Summer was blue, and wider still.
On the long slopes of dusk
we kids would mobilize
for Red Light, Green Light,
Hide and Seek—Oliver Avenue commandos
daring as kamikazes because it was war
and we weren't there. When
it turned dark, we stopped the game:
Oley, oley, all in free!
Somewhere our fathers were dying
to hear those words.

We slept like fluttering birds.
We sank through the waters of night
and swam to where our fathers lay
to touch their half-known faces.
I watch the youngest dreamer
diving to that sea's dark center
where she will find
words, driftwood, coral,

root and branch twining a path
she will never have to follow back
because she knows she always can.

Forget *les neiges d'antan*—
I can make it snow for her
any time she wants.

# In My Home Village

All night coyotes crooned around my bed.
This morning four school girls in hoodies

came to write poems at my kitchen table
and I was happy like an oak with acorns.

When the local fire siren sounded at noon,
horses down by the creek lifted their heads.

The afternoon was perfect. Our wet planet
kept rotating without my close supervision

while the cold North Pole and South Pole
called to each other through molten rock.

When "D" hill rolled east to block the sun,
clouds above the mountain throbbed pink.

Just now a rainbow trout swam me to bed
where the Dipper drips sleep on my eyes.

I think dying might feel like this – luscious
and complete, the tremble after the love.

## Sleepers

After martinis and supper my father dozed in a chair (a persistent
family tendency)—the best and often only sleep he'd get. His raw
exhausted mornings were buoyed by a shower and shave, the
optimism he had to invent to run his business.

Audubon boasted he could
thrive on four hours nightly, up by three to roam the woods;
perhaps he had the gene variation linked to needing scant rest?
Though failure plagued his ventures he abstained from spirits—
a vow he'd made as a youth in Nantes.

By all accounts a charmer,
yet prone like my dad to bouts of despair, Audubon lived to be
sixty-five. Demented, at the end. The arsenic some say now,
in a compound used to preserve his specimens. Who knew? But
science loves to reinterpret history.

My father drank his coffee
black. It cleared his head and hurt his gut. It was lung disease that
got him—neglecting to protect himself while insulating our attic.
The fiberglass. He'd likely have dismissed the man as shiftless—
what sort has so much time to ramble?

Else he might have marveled at the indefatigable Audubon, who took no pick-me-up but snuff when he could afford it, pausing for midmorning toast and milk. Brief but dependable sleep still many hours off. And twenty-five magnificent miles already under his belt.

*Eloise Bruce*

# A Love Affair with Extinction 2014

A Pleistocene savanna in springtime,
copses of trees with low branches
and a wooly hippopotamus.
Everyone, yes everyone, thinks it beautiful.

It turns out we are a nostalgic species.
Our favorite color is blue
with the requisite body of water,
far-off mountains
and an inviting path.

Never mind that we want the branches low
to escape the saber-tooth tiger,
never mind all that.  We long for the place
we first rose from four legs
and walked toward the vanishing point.

## After the Wedding

Tablecloths and silver put away,
living room furniture returned to place,
ordinary objects we hid for the occasion
found again—cell phone, bills.

Your father's *tallis*—the canopy over us—
folded and restored to its velvet bag,
sleeping again with my father's
the rabbi wrapped us in.

Our grown children, two and two,
holding the *chuppah* poles.

We emerge from our home to a world
spinning in fear and war, still sorrowing,
nothing changed beyond ourselves
alight with private happiness.

I reach my finger under tinfoil
and lift an aqua rosebud
from the top of leftover cake.

## The Joshua Trees

*Joshua Tree Park, California*

But their hands are only blossom,
and I can never tell
which way they're pointing.

Once I set out to woo the world,
across a continent of stone,
a court for giants,

mesas arranged like sacred vessels
holding a secret name.
I didn't know a thing

about the delicate and powerful
moves between a man and woman.
Orchard of ancestors,

I still don't understand
how we are taken by this world.
Think of how the skull bones grow,

those threadlike fracture joints,
their flexibility. Anything could break
the thin drum of the fontanelle.

# Acknowledgements

A Love Affair with Extinction. Eloise Bruce, *US 1 Worksheets*.

*Darkness, the Last Clown*. Lois Marie Harrod, *Poet Lore*.

After the Wedding. Maxine Susman, *Jewish Women's Literary Annual*.

Alchemy in the Forest of Drawn Metal. Eloise Bruce, *Grounds for Sculpture Anthology*.

At the Swimming Hole We Consider Female Body Image. Juditha Dowd, *Poetry Monday (International Psychoanalysis)*.

*August 6, l945 (Dresden)*. Juditha Dowd, *Ekphrasis*.

Caryatids. Sharon Olson. *Cider Press Review*.

Contained. Maxine Susman, *Ekphrasis*.

Cutting Clouds. Lois Marie Harrod, *Red Paint Hill Poetry Journal*.

Discovering Mildew in the Baby Clothes. Maxine Susman, *US1 Worksheets*.

Downsizing. Juditha Dowd, *Schuylkill Valley Review*.

Eve's Daughter. Maxine Susman, *Adanna*.

Fiddler Crabs. Maxine Susman, *US1 Worksheets*.

Five Ways to Grieve. Penelope Scambly Schott, *Antiphon*.

His Eyes. Penelope Scambly Schott, *The Liberal Media Made Me Do It: Poetic Responses to NPR & PBS Stories*, ed. Robbi Nester.

Large-Billed Reed Warblers. Juditha Dowd, *Exit 13*.

from *Nightmares of the Minor Poet*. Lois Marie Harrod, *Off the Coast*.

Hooks. Juditha Dowd, *Journal of New Jersey Poets*.

Lady Slippers. Maxine Susman, *Tower Poets*.

*Like a Maelstrom with a Notch*. Lois Marie Harrod, *Naugatuck River Review*.

Lucid Dreaming. Juditha Dowd, *Journal of New Jersey Poets*.

Mayflower Landing. Maxine Susman, *Off the Coast*.

Motley Fool. Sharon Olson, *Off the Coast*.

My Dog Lily. Penelope Scambly Schott, *Nimrod.*

No Breath, No Smut. Sharon Olson, *Off the Coast.*

Nowadays. Judy Rowe Michaels, *New Ohio Review.*

Paroxysms. Sharon Olson, *Off the Coast.*

*Pulvis et umbra sumus.* Lois Marie Harrod, *The Stillwater Review.*

Self-Portrait, Provincelands. Maxine Susman, *Provincelands* (Finishing Line Press).

*Show Me How to Survive Under a Heating Vent.* Penelope Scambly Schott, *US 1 Worksheets.*

Sleepers. Juditha Dowd, *The Stillwater Review.*

Spring Rain. Judy Rowe Michaels, *Journal of New Jersey Poets.*

That Day. Sharon Olson, *Arroyo Literary Review.*

The Legend of the Straw Heart. Lois Marie Harrod, *And She Took the Heart* (Casa de Cinco Hermanas).

The Miraculous Draught of Fishes. Sharon Olson, *String Poet.*

The Sacred and the Profane. Sharon Olson*, Organs of Vision and Speech Magazine.*

The Spineless. Lois Marie Harrod, *Fourth River.*

The Woman Who Lost Her Heart. Lois Marie Harrod, *And She Took the Heart* (Casa de Cinco Hermanas).

The Two Cakes. Sharon Olson, *California Quarterly.*

Thinking Ahead. Penelope Scambly Schott, *Miramar.*

What Can Travel Faster Than the Speed of Light? Eloise Bruce, *Caesura.*

Worst Fire Season on Record. Penelope Scambly Schott, *Timberline Review.*

# Bios

**Eloise Bruce** is the author of *Rattle* from CavenKerry Press. She is a recovering theater artist and founder of Idaho Theater for Youth. She currently works as a teaching artist with Playwright's Theater of New Jersey and Young Audiences. She is the youth editor of *RavensPerch Literary Magazine* and lives with her husband the poet David Keller.

**Juditha Dowd** writes poetry, essays and fiction. Recent work has been published in *Kestrel, Schuylkill Valley Review, Off the Coast, Canary, Spillway* and *Ekphrasis*, as well as featured on *Poetry Daily* and *Verse Daily*. She has authored three chapbooks of poems and a full-length collection, *Mango in Winter*.

**Lois Marie Harrod** sixteenth poetry collection, *Nightmares of the Minor Poet*, was published by Five Oaks Press, 2016. *Fragments from the Biography of Nemesis* appeared in 2013. A Geraldine R. Dodge poet, she teaches part time at The College of New Jersey. For online bio and work, see www.loismariehar-rod.org.

**Betty Bonham Lies** is the author of three volumes of poetry and four other books. She is the senior poetry editor of *US 1 Worksheets*. A Geraldine R. Dodge poet, she also teaches at the Princeton Senior Resource Center.

**Judy Rowe Michaels,** former poet in residence at Princeton Day School and a Geraldine R. Dodge poet, has three poetry collections, most recently the chapbook *Ghost Notes,* and three books on teaching writing. She gives talks on ovarian cancer to medical schools for Survivors Teaching Students and presents on poetry at conferences.

**Sharon Olson** is a native Californian and retired librarian. She moved to Lawrenceville, New Jersey in 2012. Her book *The Long Night of Flying* was published by Sixteen Rivers Press in 2006. Her poems have appeared in such journals as *String Poet, The Curator, Arroyo Literary Review, Off the Coast,* and *Cider Press Review.*

**Penelope Scambly Schott**'s verse biography *A is for Anne: Mistress Hutchinson Disturbs the Commonwealth* received the Oregon Book Award for Poetry. Her most recent book is *How I Became an Historian.* Penelope lives in Portland and Dufur, Oregon, where she teaches an annual workshop.

**Maxine Susman** has published six chapbooks, most recently *Provincelands* (2016), set on Cape Cod. Other books take place in the Catskill Mountains, Northern Ontario, and Occupied France. She teaches poetry writing and fiction through the Osher Lifelong Learning Institute of Rutgers University.

**Gretna Wilkinson,** born and raised in Guyana, South America, began her teaching career as a missionary teacher in the jungles there. She has published five chapbooks and a full-length collection *Opening the Drawer* (Cool Women Press). Dodge Poet, Monmouth County Arts Educator of the Year (2012) and Red Bank Regional Teacher of the Year (2015), she is founder and editor-in-chief of *The Ravens Perch,* www.theravensperch.com.